"I am the light of the world: he that followeth me shall not walk in darkness, but shall have the light of life."

Jesus Christ

John 8:12 KJV

Helpful hints:

- For a special *ARTISTIC* touch, try using **watercolor** pencils.

- Employing a **chalk medium or fluorescent gel pens** for pictures with a black background add an alluring 'pop.'

- Be sure to **place a sheet of paper between** pictures when coloring with pens.

RELIABLE REFERENCE POINT

BRANDED GOODS

lighthouse

1978 ★ ★ ★

EAST COAST

BRANDED GOODS

TROUBLED WATER

LIGHTHOUSE

PACIFIC OCEAN

1978

BRANDED GOODS

LIGHTHOUSE

TROUBLED WATER

PACIFIC OCEAN

TROUBLED WATER

lighthouse

★ ★ ★

EAST COAST
BRANDED GOODS

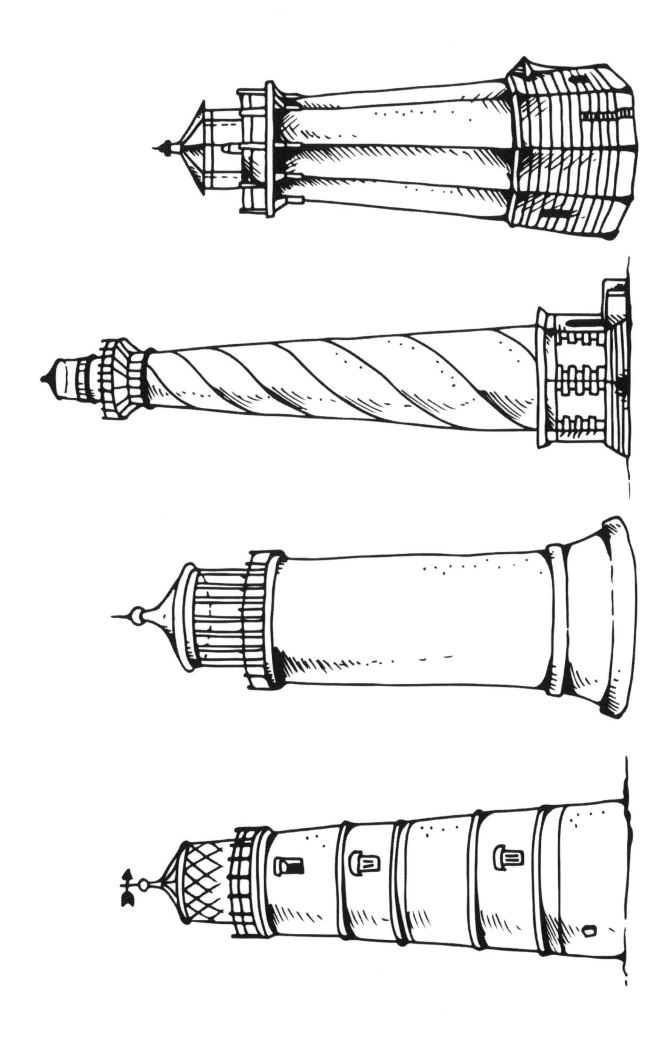

SHARK
9 8
1989
COLLEGE TEAM

FIRE
Camp
1998

GREEN CLUB
96

BRANDED GOODS
CAMP
1999

EXPLORE
SINCE 1996

YACHT
CLUB 96

FOREST
1998 2015
Camp

LIGHTHOUSE
SINCE 1996

NEW YORK
8 9
COLLEGE TEAM

Nautical collection

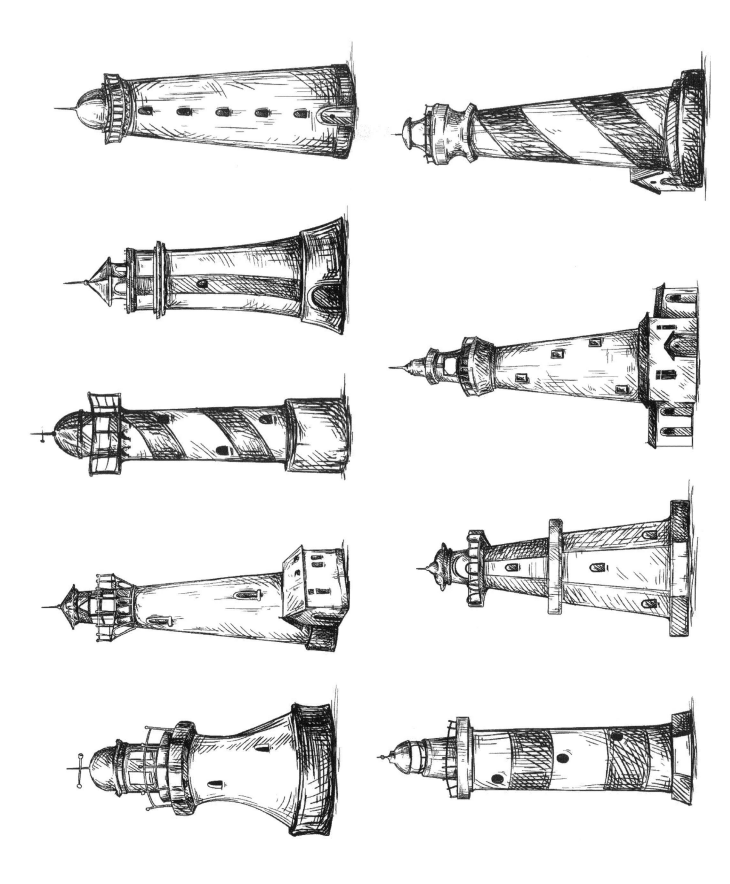

ocean

sail

beach

coast

sea

nautical collection

Lighthouse

to the lighthouse

LIGHTHOUSE

LOREM
LIGHTHOUSE
IPSUM

LightHouse

LightHouse

LIGHT
HOUSE

LIGHTHOUSE

LIGHTHOUSE

LIGHTHOUSE

LIGHTHOUSE

WINTER IS COMING

If you've enjoyed this adult coloring book, please see our other titles and kindly consider leaving a review.

Thanks for coloring!

Made in the USA
San Bernardino, CA
09 March 2018